W9-APX-910

ANCIENT CIVILIZATIONS

Aztecs

By Tami Deedrick

Raintree Steck-Vaughn Publishers

A Harcourt Company

Austin · New York

www.steck-vaughn.com

Copyright © 2002, Steck-Vaughn Company

All rights reserved. No part of this book may be reproduced or utilized in any form or by any means, electronic or mechanical, including photocopying, recording, or by any information storage and retrieval system, without permission in writing from the publisher. Inquiries should be addressed to Copyright Permissions, Steck-Vaughn Company, P.O. Box 26015, Austin, TX 78755.

Published by Raintree Steck-Vaughn Publishers,
an imprint of Steck-Vaughn Company.

Library of Congress Cataloging-in-Publication Data
Aztecs/by Tami Deedrick.
p.cm.—(Ancient civilizations)
Includes bibliographical references and index.
ISBN 0-7398-3579-3
1. Aztecs—Juvenile literature. [1.Aztecs. 2. Indians of Mexico.] I. Title.
II. Ancient civilizations (Raintree Steck-Vaughn)
F1219.73 .D43 2001
972'.018 21

2001019204

Printed and bound in the United States of America
1 2 3 4 5 6 7 8 9 10 WZ 05 04 03 02 01

Produced by Compass Books

Photo Acknowledgments
Corbis/Gianni Dagli Orti, 9, 33; Jacqui Hurst, 16; Richard A. Cooke, 29;
   Charles & Josette Lenars, 34; Bettmann, 40
Root Resources/Loren M. Root, title page; Tony Root, 25
Unicorn Stock Photos/Phyllis Kedl, 15
Visuals Unlimited/Kjell B. Sandved, 12; D. Cavagnaro, 19; Dick Keen, 20;
   Robin Karpan, 22; N. Pecnik, 26; Francis and Donna Caldwell, 30;
   John D. Cunningham, 36, 39; Jo Pratzer, 43

Content Consultants
Dr. Michael Smith
Professor, Department of Anthropology
Director, Institute for Mesoamerican Studies
University of New York at Albany (SUNY)

Don L. Curry
Educational Author, Editor, Consultant, and Columnist

UC BR
J
F1219
.73
.D43
2002

Contents

Land of the Aztecs

Gulf of Mexico

Lake Texcoco

Tlaltelolco

Tenochtitlàn

MEXICO

Pacific Ocean

LEGEND

 Aztec Civilization

Surrounding Land

● Cities

Water

Aztec History

Mexico City, Mexico, sits on top of a lot of history. From about A.D. 1325 to 1519, a powerful group of people called Aztecs lived on the land where this city is built.

The area the Aztecs ruled covered about 125,000 square miles (201,168 square km). The center of the Aztec world was Tenochtitlàn. The Aztecs built this great city on an island in Lake Texcoco, which is in the Valley of Mexico. This valley lies between the Gulf of Mexico and the Pacific Ocean.

The Aztecs controlled the area where they lived for about 200 years. They ruled at least three million people.

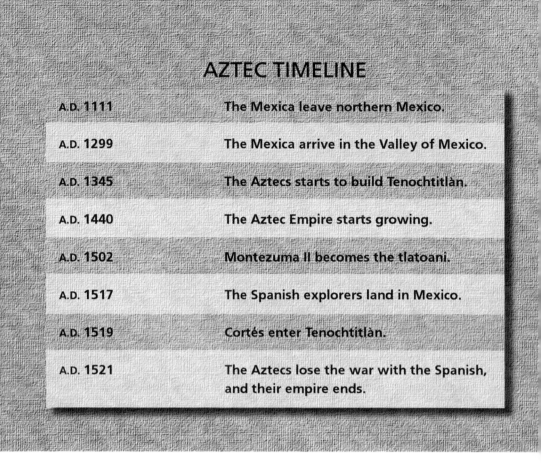

AZTEC TIMELINE

A.D. **1111**	The Mexica leave northern Mexico.
A.D. **1299**	The Mexica arrive in the Valley of Mexico.
A.D. **1345**	The Aztecs starts to build Tenochtitlàn.
A.D. **1440**	The Aztec Empire starts growing.
A.D. **1502**	Montezuma II becomes the tlatoani.
A.D. **1517**	The Spanish explorers land in Mexico.
A.D. **1519**	Cortés enter Tenochtitlàn.
A.D. **1521**	The Aztecs lose the war with the Spanish, and their empire ends.

Beginnings

The Aztecs were once a tribe called Mexica that lived in northern Mexico. They believed in Huitzilopochtli, the god of the Sun and war. The Aztecs said that in the 12th century, Huitzilopochtli sent them on a long trip to central Mexico. Huitzilopochtli said that he would send them a sign when they reached a good place to live. The sign was an eagle sitting on top of a cactus and eating a snake. In the 13th century, the Aztecs saw this sign near Lake Texcoco, so they moved there.

By the time the Aztecs arrived, there were already many city-states in the Lake Texcoco area. A city-state is a tiny nation built around a central town. When the Aztecs first reached Lake Texcoco, people from a larger city-state called Azcapotzalco made the Aztecs serve them. Some Aztecs escaped to an island in the middle of Lake Texcoco and began building Tenochtitlàn.

In 1428, the Aztecs took over Azcapotzalco. With their new freedom, the Aztecs became a leading city-state. They made their capital city of Tenochtitlàn larger. They also became an ally to two other powerful city-states. An ally is a person or country that helps another in a time of need. With the help of their allies, the Aztecs took over many other city-states.

Government

A god-like king called the **tlatoani**, or "The One Who Speaks," ruled the Aztecs. The tlatoani was in charge of religion, the army, and courts of law. People visiting the tlatoani wore plain blankets and bowed down before him. They walked out of the room backwards because it was against the law to turn one's back to the king. The tlatoani did not leave his palace very often. When he did, he was carried through the town, and the people could not look at him.

The tlatoani had a group of advisors who were in charge of different jobs. An advisor is someone who gives ideas about how to run things. For their help, the king gave his advisors land, homes, and money. The tlatoani's top advisor was a man called Snake Woman. Snake Woman was the chief judge and was in charge of most of Tenochtitlàn.

The tlatoani had **priests** to help him. Priests were men who served the gods and worked in the **temples**. A temple is a building for

▲ Aztec priests read calendar stones like this
one to tell which day it was.

serving the gods. Priests planned the calendar
and told the people how to worship the gods.

The Aztec government divided its people
into villages called **calpullis**. Each paid taxes to
the tlatoani. There were about 100 families in
each calpulli. Each calpulli had a school and a
certain amount of land for farming.

Words to Say

calmecac (kahl-MAY-kahk)
calpulli (kahl-POH-lee)
chinampa (chin-AHM-pah)
Huitzilopochtli (weet-see-loh-POHCH-tlee)
Nahuatl (nah-WAH-tl)
Quetzalcoatl (kayt-zal-COH-atl)
Tenochtitlàn (tay-noch-tee-TLAHN)
Texcoco (tesh-KOH-koh)
Tlatoani (tlah-toh-AH-nee)

The Aztec Army

War was an important part of Aztec life. Aztecs fought to protect their city or to capture other city-states. They needed payments, or **tributes**, from other people to keep their city running smoothly. Tributes included blankets, clothes, gold, weapons, feathers, food, and pottery. Pottery is objects made out of hardened clay, such as jars, plates, bowls, and cups.

All Aztec men served in the army. As boys, they went to special schools to learn how to fight. There, professional officers taught them how to take prisoners and use weapons. The Aztecs believed that the best warriors were those who captured the most prisoners. An Aztec boy was not considered a man until he captured his first prisoner.

Aztec warriors hurt their enemies' legs so that the enemies could be taken as prisoners. Prisoners were then taken back to Tenochtitlàn as slaves. A slave is a person owned by someone else.

Warriors wore armor made of padded cotton. They soaked the cotton in saltwater until it was stiff. Sometimes Aztecs carried wooden shields covered with leather and feathers. Special warriors who captured many prisoners wore special outfits that looked like an eagle or a large wildcat called a jaguar.

This clay statue shows what an Aztec noble looked like.

Daily Life of the Aztecs

There were three main **classes** of Aztec people. The nobles were the highest class. They lived in large houses and owned land. Only nobles could serve as priests, government workers, or advisors. Some warriors who showed great skill in war became nobles, too.

Most of the Aztecs were working people, or the middle class. They were farmers or craftspeople. They served in the army when the tlatoani declared war.

Slaves were the lowest class of Aztecs. Some slaves were prisoners of war, criminals, or people who owed others money.

Clothing

Aztecs had laws about what people could wear. The working-class people and slaves wore plain, simple clothes. Cloth was made of fibers, or threads, from the maguey plant. Nobles wore colorful cotton clothes decorated with feathers or gold. They wore feather hats and many kinds of jewelry. Nobles also wore gold necklaces, earrings, bracelets, and rings in their lips and noses.

Working-class men wore **loincloths**. These long strips of cloth wrapped around the waist, pulled through the legs, and tied in front. They also wore a sleeveless cloak tied over their right shoulder. A cloak is a cloth placed around the shoulders. If the cloak fell below the knees, the man was put to death. It was against the law for working-class people to wear long cloaks.

Noble men also wore loincloths and cloaks, but their cloaks were tied in front and fell below the knees. Sometimes they wore more than one cloak to show how rich they were.

This painting shows how Aztecs dressed.

Women wore long skirts and long, sleeveless blouses. They covered their faces with brightly colored make-up. They painted their bodies yellow, blue, green, or red. Sometimes they colored their faces with axin, a yellow cream made from insects. They also stained their teeth red.

Aztecs decorated their homes with colorful
hangings and with rugs like this one.

Homes

The tlatoani's palace was at the center of
the city. It was two levels high and had more
than 50 rooms. One room was for his throne,
and the others were for his advisors. A large
garden full of colorful flowers grew around
the palace.

Houses belonging to rich nobles surrounded the palace. Only nobles could build houses with two levels. An open courtyard circled by high stone or adobe walls surrounded most houses. Adobe is a mud or clay brick dried in the sun. Flowers covered the flat roofs. Inside the noble houses were many rooms for sleeping, eating, and cooking. Other rooms were for servants. Curtains hung in the doorways. Small bells on the curtains made noise if someone came in the house.

Working-class people lived on the outer edge of town. By law, their houses could only be one level with two rooms. One room was for cooking and eating, and the other room was for sleeping. The houses were usually made of mud bricks. Sometimes a blanket hung in the outer doorway. Working-class people had no furniture. Most Aztecs slept on mats on the ground and covered themselves with blankets if it got cold.

Food

Maize, or corn, was the most important food for Aztecs. They also planted squash, avocados, peppers, and tomatoes.

After working for awhile, Aztecs ate their first meal of the day. It was usually atole, a soup-like dish made from corn. They sweetened the atole with honey or spiced it with peppers. In the hottest part of the day, the Aztecs had their second meal. They ate flat corn pancakes called **tortillas**. The Aztecs wrapped the tortillas around beans, tomatoes, and peppers. The last meal was atole at bedtime.

Meat was not a big part of the Aztec diet, but sometimes they ate turkey, fish, and dog. Rich Aztecs dined on crab, oysters, and turtle.

Aztecs had no stoves. To cook, they put three stones around a small fire. They put food on a flat, clay plate called a comalli that sat on the stones.

▲ The Aztecs used peppers to flavor many of their dishes.

Rich Aztecs enjoyed a special cold drink made from cacao beans. It was called chocolatl, or chocolate. Sometimes they used vanilla, spices, or honey to flavor the chocolatl. The poor drank mostly water.

Aztec artists carved this animal into the side of one of their temples.

Art

Aztecs created art to show how powerful their gods and **empire** were. An empire is a group of countries that all have the same ruler. Aztecs made most of their art from huge blocks of stone. Aztec artists were skilled at using simple tools to carve detailed statues of gods, rulers, animals, and warriors. To decorate the outside of important buildings, they carved pictures of animals and battles into stone blocks. Aztecs also made special stone bowls and cups for their temples. These things looked like shells, plants, or special animals.

Gold was another important part of Aztec arts, crafts, and jewelry. Workers used gold to make masks for religious events. They also used gold to make necklaces, earrings, nose rings, and arm bands for nobles. It was against the law for working-class people to wear gold jewelry.

Aztecs carved obsidian into different shapes to make jewelry. Obsidian is a black glass from volcanoes. Rich nobles used flat pieces of obsidian as mirrors.

Aztec Building

The most important Aztec buildings were **pyramid**-shaped temples. Aztec pyramids had rectangle bases and four sloping sides. Staircases led up the sides to a flat platform on top. A shrine, or a place built to honor a special god, was on top of the pyramid.

Aztecs made their own houses from wood, but built temples from rock so the buildings would last. They shaped the rocks and fit them together into pyramids and buildings.

One of the most famous Aztec buildings is the Great Temple. This pyramid is more than 200 feet (61 m) tall. Two tall staircases lead up the front to two shrines at the top. One shrine honors the god of rain. Another shrine honors the god of the Sun and war.

Many smaller temples and religious buildings surrounded the Great Temple. Some of these buildings had unusual shapes. Quetzalcoatl was the god of the priests. His temple was shaped like a circle and surrounded by rock coils that looked like a

▲ This is a model of the Great Temple and the surrounding buildings.

snake's body. Schools to train priests and warriors were also in the temple area.

A large plaza was near the temple. A plaza is an open area that often has walkways, trees, and places to sit down. The plazas were the center of activity for the Aztecs.

Aztecs carved stones with glyphs.

Music

The Aztecs loved music and dancing. They wrote poetry and songs about life. Aztecs made drums out of wood or clay. They covered the drums with animal skins. Aztecs used wood or reeds to make flutes and whistles. They made rattles from bones or shells.

Aztecs performed many songs and dances at religious ceremonies. Movements in the dances told a story about their history or gods. Dancing and singing was a way to make the gods happy. Then, the Aztecs believed their gods would make crops grow.

Glyphs and Nahuatl

Aztecs spoke a language called **Nahuatl**, which did not have an alphabet. Aztecs told stories to pass their culture down to their children. They also learned how to write in word pictures called **glyphs**. The pictures stood for words. For example, footprints meant travel. A scroll coming out of a person's mouth meant talking. The glyphs also showed plants, animals, and weapons. Sometimes Aztecs put two or more pictures together to show one word.

Some Aztec books called **codices** still exist. People study the codices to learn about the Aztecs. Codex is the single form of codices. A codex was made from a long strip of paper. The paper was folded like a fan.

School

Aztec children started learning very young. By age three, children learned how to do work around the house. By 14, boys could paddle a canoe, fish, and help with farming. Girls could cook, weave cloth, and make clothes.

Both boys and girls went to a school called the House of Song. There, they learned songs, poems, dances, and how to play instruments.

Male children of the nobles went to a temple school called a calmecac to learn how to be a government worker. Priests taught them about Aztec laws, history, religion, calendars, medicine, and writing.

Male children of the working-class went to a school called telpochcalli. People from their calpulli taught them Aztec laws, history, and religion. They also taught them how to fight and other skills they needed for jobs.

Aztec girls were mostly taught at home by their mothers. They learned how to spin

▲ **Aztec boys learned how to play musical instruments like this drum.**

thread into cloth and how to cook. Some noble girls worked in the temple for a year before getting married. A few noble girls became priestesses. Priestesses are women who serve their gods by working in the temples.

This is an ancient Aztec pyramid. It was built so well that it is still standing today.

What Did the Aztecs Do?

The Aztecs were excellent builders. They turned a small island into a huge city. Many of their huge stone buildings are still standing today.

The Aztecs lived by firm rules. They set up courts for those who did not follow the rules. For small crimes, criminals had to pay the person they had wronged. A criminal is someone who breaks the law. If criminals could not pay, they had to become slaves until the money was paid. For big crimes, the criminal was usually put to death. The rules kept crime very low in Aztec culture. Tenochtitlàn was a safe place to live.

Chinampas

One of the greatest successes of the Aztec people was the **chinampa,** which was a small human-made island. To make a chinampa, Aztecs used dirt and mud to build sections of land in the water. They held the dirt and mud in place with a frame. Then, they planted willow trees in the corners. The roots grew deep and kept the garden in one place.

Chinampas could be as small as 5 feet (1.5 m) across and 50 feet (15 m) long. But most were about 30 feet (9 m) across and 300 feet (91 m) long.

The Aztecs built houses on the chinampas. They also planted crops, such as maize, beans, and squash. Sometimes they changed crops every year. One year, they might plant maize. The next year, they might plant tomatoes. Changing crops kept the soil healthy. Aztecs also planted flowers on chinampas.

▲ This painting shows how Aztecs built chinampas to grow crops on.

Canals of water ran between the chinampas. A canal is a waterway made by people. The Aztecs traveled around the city in canoes. They scooped the water from the canals to water the plants growing on the chinampas.

This painting shows how Aztec homes surrounded the temples in Tenochtitlàn.

Tenochtitlàn

In the 1500s, the city of Tenochtitlàn was one of the greatest cities in the world. **Archaeologists** think about 250,000 people lived there.

The Aztecs planned their city very well. They set up the streets in square blocks. Roads were straight and ran north to south or west to east. The main street ran from east to west to show the way the Sun travels through the sky.

Aztecs built **aqueducts** to bring water to the city. An aqueduct is a pipe or channel built to carry water from one place to another. Aqueducts brought water from mountain springs into Aztec cities. Most aqueducts were above the ground.

The Aztecs also had large markets where people bought and sold goods. About 60,000 people shopped in the town markets every day. People bought and sold food, clothes, and goods the merchants had bought in other cities. Judges sat in the markets to settle any fights. Inspectors walked through the markets to make sure no one was being cheated.

Spanish explorers wanted the Aztec's riches, such as these gold objects.

How Do We Know?

In 1517, Hernando Cortés and a group of 500 Spanish soldiers landed in Mexico. In 1519, the Spanish met the Aztecs. Montezuma II was the ruler of the Aztecs when Cortés came. Montezuma thought Cortés looked like an Aztec god. Montezuma sent gold and other gifts to Cortés.

To get more gold, Cortés captured Montezuma and started a war with the Aztecs in 1521. Some Aztecs died in the war. Many others died from smallpox, a sickness the Spanish brought. In only three months, the Spanish took over the great Aztec empire. The Aztecs were forced to serve the Spaniards.

Learning About the Aztecs

The Aztecs lived long ago. No one alive today saw the great empire. Still, we can learn about it using three main sources of information.

The first source is the Aztec codices. Most of the codices were destroyed by the Spanish. However, the Spanish did send some back home to Spain. These books are still in European libraries. People can study the codices and see how the Aztecs lived.

Another source is reports from the Spanish. One soldier named Bernal Diaz wrote a book called *The Conquest of New Spain*. Diaz describes the wars with the Aztecs and the things he saw in the city. Cortés also wrote letters to the king of Spain. Missionaries came to Mexico after Spain claimed the land. A missionary is someone sent from a church to teach people about his or her religion. Missionaries also wrote about the Aztecs.

The third way we know about the Aztecs is from the ruins of their great city,

▲ **Archaeologists study Aztec artifacts like this pottery bowl.**

Tenochtitlàn. Scientists called archaeologists study the ruins to learn about the Aztecs. Archaeologists study the past.

Archaeologists also find and study Aztec **artifacts**, such as pots. An artifact is an object that was made or used by people in the past. Artifacts show how the Aztecs lived.

People found these Aztec ruins when they began building a subway in Mexico.

Aztec Sites and Artifacts

People in Mexico have found many Aztec ruins. Archaeologists explore them and sometimes rebuild them. People from Mexico and from other countries travel to see the sites and the artifacts.

Another Aztec city named Tlaltelolco is being dug up. Archaeologists have found parts of a temple and an aqueduct.

Mexico City is famous for its National Museum of Anthropology. Anthropology is the study of people and their cultures. This museum has the largest collection of ancient American artifacts in the world. Ancient means old. One room of the museum is all about the Aztecs. The museum workers have recreated some Aztec sights. Visitors can also see Aztec calendars, jewelry, art, and pottery.

 The Aztec people played two games that are very much like games played today. One was called tlatchli. It was like basketball and soccer mixed together. They tried to get a small rubber ball into a hoop. Players could only hit the ball with their knees, hips, or elbows. They could not use their hands. The hoop was turned so that the opening was on the side instead of the top. The game ended when someone got the ball through the hoop. Another game was patolli. It was a board game played with beans marked with white dots. The beans were like our dice.

Aztecs in the Modern World

Today, about 100 million people live in Mexico. Some of them are from the families of the Aztecs. About one million people still speak the Aztec language, Nahuatl.

Some modern Aztecs still live like the Aztecs of old. These people are called Nahua. They follow Aztec ways and celebrate special Aztec religious events with singing and dancing.

This dancer is performing Aztec dances at a Native American powwow, or gathering.

aqueduct (AK-wuh-duhkt)—a pipe or channel built to carry water from one place to another

archaeologist (ar-kee-OL-uh-jist)—a scientist who studies ruins to learn about the past

architecture (AR-ki-tek-chur)—the style and way a building is made

artifact (ART-uh-fakt)—an object that was made or used by humans in the past

calpulli (cahl-POH-lee)—a village made up of a group of Aztec families

chinampa (chee-NAM-pah)—a small island made by people

class (KLASS)—a group of people in a society who have similar jobs

codices (KO-di-seez)—ancient books that help us learn about ancient cultures

culture (KUHL-chur)—the way of life, ideas, customs, and traditions of a group of people

empire (EM-pire)—a group of countries with
one ruler
glyphs (GLIFSS)—pictures that stand for
words and objects
loincloth (LOIN-klawth)—a long strip of cloth
wrapped around the waist, pulled through
the legs, and tied in front
maize (MAYZ)—corn
Nahuatl (nah-WAH-tl)—the Aztec language
priest (PREEST)—men who served the gods
and worked in temples
pyramid (PIHR-uh-mid)—a stone monument
with sloping sides
temple (TEM-puhl)—a special building used
for worshiping gods
tlatoani (tlah-toh-AH-nee)—the Aztec ruler
tortilla (tor-TEE-yah)—a round, flat, corn
pancake-like bread
tributes (TRIB-yoots)—payments made by a
group of people to their ruler

Internet Sites

Aztecs
http://library.thinkquest.org/27981/

Minnesota State University e-Museum—Aztec
http://emuseum.mankato.msus.edu/
  prehistory/latinamerica/meso/cultures/
  aztec_empire.html

Templo Mayor Museum
http://archaeology.la.asu.edu/tm/index2.htm

Useful Addresses

Embassy of Mexico
1911 Pennsylvania Avenue
Washington, DC 20006

Mexican Cultural Institute
2829 16th Street NW
Washington, DC 20009

Mexican Secretariat of Tourism
21 East 63rd Street, Third Floor
New York, NY 10021

Index